Camille Clavi

Simple Crochet Motifs

20 Patterns for Stylish Accessories

STACKPOLE
BOOKS

Acknowledgments

The editor thanks Plassard-Diffusion, which provided nearly all the yarn used in these projects.

Plassard-Diffusion—La Filature—F—71800 Varenne-sous-Dun
info@plassard-diffusion.com
www.plassard-diffusion.com

Thanks to UNIQLO and 0044
www.uniqlo.com
www.o-paris.com

Thanks also to Claire, Maya, and Violaine.

Published by
STACKPOLE BOOKS
5067 Ritter Road
Mechanicsburg, PA 17055
www.stackpolebooks.com

Printed in Romania

10 9 8 7 6 5 4 3 2 1

First edition

ISBN 978-0-8117-1276-7

Editions Larousse
Editorial director: Colette Hanicotte
Editorial coordination: Corinne de Montalembert, assisted by Chloé Cosnefroy
Photography: Ayumi Shino
Illustrations: Camille Clavi

Stackpole Books
Translation: Kathryn Fulton
Pagination: Tessa J. Sweigert
Cover design: Caroline M. Stover

Cataloging-in-publication data is on file with the Library of Congress.

Contents

The abc's of crochet

The projects in this book are all made from motifs: squares, circles, hexagons, flowers, and so on. The motifs are made individually and then assembled, either as you complete each building-block or at the end, once they all have been made.

Motif crochet uses the same basic stitches as traditional crochet. The major difference with working with motifs is that each motif starts from a short chain joined into a ring instead of a straight chain.

Holding the hook and the yarn (right-handed)

Hold the hook in your right hand like a pencil, with your thumb and index finger on either side of the tool.

Hold the yarn in your left hand and, to control the tension, pass it between your index finger and middle finger. For greater control, you can pass it between your third and fourth fingers as well.

Holding the hook and the yarn (left-handed)

Hold the hook in your left hand like a pencil, with your thumb and index finger on either side of the tool.

Hold the yarn in your right hand and, to control the tension, pass it between your index finger and middle finger. For greater control, you can pass it between your third and fourth fingers as well.

The basic stitches are explained and illustrated for right-handed crocheters. If you're left handed, you can "translate" the illustrations by placing a mirror next to them to invert them.

The slip knot

Make a loop, put the head of the crochet hook through the loop, and use the hook to pull the strand of yarn leading to the ball or skein through this loop.

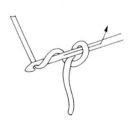

Pull both ends of the yarn to close the knot. Gently tighten the loop around the hook and place the knot underneath the hook.

Basic stitches and their symbols

O Chain

● Slip stitch

+ Single crochet

T   Half double crochet

Ŧ   Double crochet

Ŧ   Treble crochet

Ŧ   Double treble

⅄   Double crochet together

o⦿o   Picot

O   Chain (ch)

Start with a slip knot. Wrap the strand of yarn attached to the ball around the hook (this is called a yarn over and abbreviated yo).

Pull on the hook to draw the yarn through the loop. Gently tighten the knot, and you have a new chain.

To make a base chain, repeat these steps (yarn over, draw the yarn through the loop) to make the number of chains indicated in the pattern.

●   Slip stitch (sl st)

Starting with a base chain, insert the hook into the second chain from the hook, and yarn over (A). Pull the yarn through both loops on the hook (B).

+   Single crochet (sc)

Starting with a base chain, insert the hook into the second chain from the hook. Yarn over and pull the yarn through the chain (pull up a loop) (A).

Yarn over again, and pull the yarn through both loops on the hook (B).

T   Half double crochet (hdc)

Starting with a base chain, yarn over, then insert the hook into the third chain from the hook and pull up a loop (A). Yarn over again and pull the yarn through all three loops on the hook (B). At the end of the half double crochet, before starting the next stitch, there should be one loop on the hook (C).

⊤ Double crochet (dc)

Starting with a base chain, yarn over, insert the hook into the fourth chain from the hook, and pull up a loop (A). Yarn over again and pull the yarn through the first two loops on the hook (B). Yarn over a third time and pull the yarn through both of the loops on the hook (C). At the end of the double crochet, before starting the next stitch, there should be one loop on the hook (D).

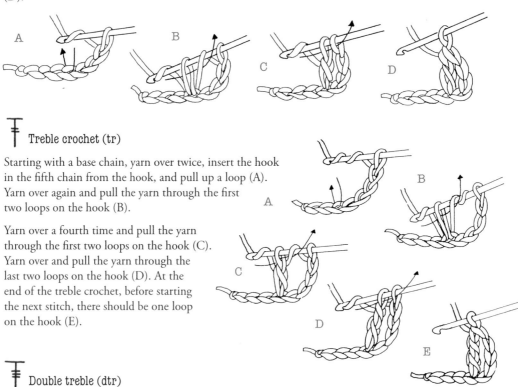

⊤ Treble crochet (tr)

Starting with a base chain, yarn over twice, insert the hook in the fifth chain from the hook, and pull up a loop (A). Yarn over again and pull the yarn through the first two loops on the hook (B).

Yarn over a fourth time and pull the yarn through the first two loops on the hook (C). Yarn over and pull the yarn through the last two loops on the hook (D). At the end of the treble crochet, before starting the next stitch, there should be one loop on the hook (E).

⊤ Double treble (dtr)

Starting with a base chain, yarn over three times, then insert the hook into the sixth chain from the hook and pull up a loop (A). Yarn over and pull the yarn through the first two loops on the hook (B).

Yarn over a fifth time and pull the yarn through the first two loops on the hook again (C). Yarn over and pull through the first two loops on the hook again; repeat one more time to finish the stitch (D).

At the end of the double treble, before starting the next stitch, there should be one loop on the hook (E).

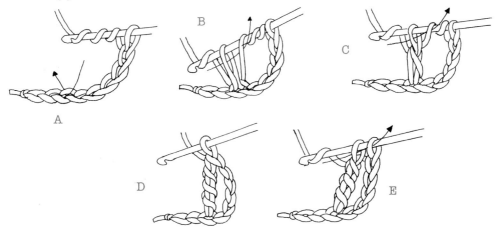

 Double crochet together (dc tog)

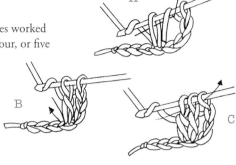

This stitch is made of at least two double crochet stitches worked together—in the projects in this book it's often three, four, or five stitches worked together. If it is made of two stitches worked together, it's written dc2tog; for three stitches, it's dc3tog; and so on. You can also work multiples of any other stitch from single crochet to double treble together.

Dc2tog:

Starting from a base chain, yarn over, insert the hook in the fourth chain from the hook, and pull up a loop; yarn over and pull the yarn through the first two loops (A). Leaving the remaining two loops on the hook, yarn over again and insert the hook into the chain again (the pattern will tell you whether to make the second stitch in the same stitch as before or in the next stitch), pull up another loop, and pull the yarn through that loop and the next, as before (B). You should have three loops on the hook at this point. Yarn over once more and pull the yarn through all the loops on the hook (C).

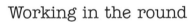 Picot (p)

A picot is a little loop of chains worked into the top of the previous row.

Start by working the base stitch (in this case, a sc, but the pattern will always indicate what kind of stitch).

To make the picot, chain three, then insert the hook into the top of the stitch the chains started from (A). Yarn over, then pull the yarn through all the loops on the hook (B).

You can also make picots with four or five chains. All the picots in this book will be three-chain picots unless the instructions say otherwise.

Working in the round

This method of crocheting allows you to create motifs in any shape—circular, square, triangular, hexagonal, and more—all starting from a simple ring of chains.

Make a chain of the length indicated in the pattern. Make a ring by working a slip stitch in the first chain (A).

On your first round, you will need to make some chains before making your first stitch (here, three; the pattern will say how many in each case). After this point, all the stitches of the first round are worked through the middle of the ring (instead of through the chains), unless the pattern says otherwise.

At the end of each round, close the round by working a slip stitch into the last of the set of chains made at the beginning of the round (C).

On the following rounds, carefully follow the instructions, which will indicate what stitches to make and where to put them (D).

Since motifs are made from one side only, never turned, they have a right side and a wrong side. It's important, when assembling a project made of motifs, to turn all the motifs to the same side.

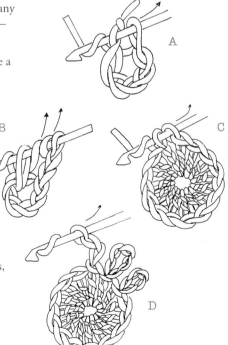

Changing yarn

To change colors or join a new ball of yarn, insert the hook into the next stitch (A). Yarn over with the old and new yarns together. Pull the yarns through the stitch and through the loop on the hook (B). Continue with the pattern, working with the new yarn.

Stopping

To finish a piece, at the end of the last row or round, cut the yarn and pull the end through the loop. Pull to gently tighten. Weave the leftover end of yarn into the back of the piece.

Assembling motifs

The best way to assemble a project made of motifs depends on the project and the shapes of the pieces; each pattern will indicate the method of assembly you should use.

Picot method

With this method, each motif is attached to the previous ones by the picots on the edges. After you make the first chain for the picot, insert the crochet hook through the loop of the picot on the motif you want to attach the one in progress to. Then finish making the picot as you normally would.

Crochet method

Place the motifs to be assembled one on top of the other, with right sides together. Insert the hook through the edge stitches of both motifs at once, and make a single crochet. Continue in this manner, working along the entire length of the edge to be attached.

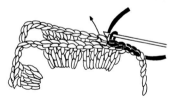

Sewing method

Place the pieces to be assembled next to each other, with the right sides up. Sew the edges together with a yarn needle, going stitch by stitch along the edges of the pieces, alternately from right to left and left to right.

How to read the patterns

Abbreviations

The patterns in this book use standard crochet abbreviations as well as symbol charts. You'll need to learn these abbreviations in order to easily read the patterns. Here is a list of the abbreviations most commonly used in this book.

ch = chain	RS = right side
ch-[number] = a chain of the length given	sc = single crochet
dc = double crochet	sk = skip
dc2tog = double crochet 2 sts together	sl st = slip stitch
dec = decrease	sp = space (as in ch-3 sp)
dtr = double treble	st(s) = stitches
hdc = half double crochet	tog = together
p = picot (of 3 ch unless otherwise specified)	tr = treble crochet
prev = previous	WS = wrong side
rnd(s) = round(s)	yo = yarn over

The symbols

The symbols in the stitch charts represent stitches or groups of stitches and are the standard international symbols for crochet charts. It is useful to learn this system, which allows you to quickly see how the motif goes together and read charted patterns from all over the world, even if the patterns themselves are not translated.

The symbol for each stitch is given with the instructions for the stitch (pages 4 and 5).

Asterisks

As you read a pattern, you may come across the * symbol. Asterisks are used to indicate repetition. Within a row, the stitches to be repeated are enclosed (at one or both ends) between asterisks. For example: "*Ch1, sk next 3 sts, 2 dc in next st. Repeat from * to the end of the row." Be careful to repeat all of the steps between the asterisks.

Often the beginning and end of the row are slightly different from the middle and are given before and after the repeated section.

Parentheses

Parentheses are also used to signal repetition. The stitches between the parentheses should be repeated the number of times indicated by the instructions. For example: "Work (1 dc, ch3, 1 dc) three times in this space." Parentheses are used when the items to be repeated form a unit.

The list of materials

The list of materials gives the amount and kind of yarn needed for a project, as well as the size of hook recommended.

The size of the garments

Pattern sizes don't always match department store sizes. Make sure the measurements given in the pattern for the finished garment match the size you want.

Making a swatch

If you're not familiar with the pattern or the stitches used in it, you should make a single instance of the motif as a swatch before starting the project to get familiar with the stitches. For projects where the dimensions of the finished garment are important, it is very important to make a swatch to check the gauge (to see if the size of your crocheting matches the size given in the pattern). If your gauge swatch is different from the size given, you need to adjust your hook size:

If your swatch is larger than the size given, you are crocheting more loosely than the person who made the pattern. Use a smaller hook to compensate.

If your swatch is smaller than the size given, you are crocheting more tightly than the person who made the pattern. Try a larger hook size.

The yarn label

The label on a skein of yarn gives you a great deal of information. Here you can find the thickness of the yarn, the kind of fiber it is made from, the weight and/or length of the skein, the recommended hook size, the color name or number, and the dye lot. This last piece of information is very important; if you run out of yarn and need to buy more, you will need to try to find yarn from the same dye lot as what you started with for the colors to match exactly. Hang on to all this information; save your yarn label!

Tools

Crochet hooks

A crochet hook is just about the only tool you need to make the projects in this book: You'll use it for all the stitches, borders, finishing, and sometimes even assembly.

Crochet hooks are available in many different sizes to correspond with different yarn weights and pattern requirements. The size can be found on the hook itself. A recommended hook size is usually found on the label of a skein of yarn, but you should always check your gauge to be sure the hook you're using will give you the size and tension you want.

Craft stores and online suppliers sell crochet hooks in many different sizes and materials.

The most widely available material for crochet hooks is metal. The smooth surface of a metal hook allows the stitches to slide easily. The smallest metal hooks are ideal for making lace. Metal is a solid and stiff material that is not easily bent or warped. Metal hooks are good tools for beginners and will last a long time. They usually have a flattened area in the middle of the hook where you can place your thumb and index finger. Others have a plastic or rubber sleeve to give you a firm grip on the tool.

Bamboo crochet hooks also have a smooth surface, and many crocheters find them very pleasant to use. Bamboo hooks are generally found in sizes C/2 (2.75 mm) through N/15 (10.0 mm).

Plastic hooks are more fragile than bamboo or metal ones and can twist or even snap when working with stiff, strong yarns. They are better for using with bulky yarns with some give. They are not recommended for crocheters who tend to work tightly, because the points of these hooks will not easily penetrate the stitches in previous rows.

The very smallest crochet hooks are only made from steel. These tiny hooks, 3.5 mm and smaller, are used for making lace and have a different numbering system from the one used for regular hooks. In the steel hook system, the smallest numbers correspond to the largest hooks, and the smallest hooks have the largest size numbers.

Most hooks sold today have both the US size and the metric size on them (or on their packaging)—but if you come across one that only has the metric size, the table on the next page will help you determine the size you need. As there is sometimes overlap between US sizes, the hook sizes recommended for the projects in this book will be given in both US size and millimeters.

Crochet hook sizes

Regular Hooks		Steel Hooks	
US Size	Metric Size	US Size	Metric Size
S	19 mm	00	3.5 mm
Q	16 mm	0	3.25 mm
P/Q	15 mm	1	2.75 mm
N/P-15	10 mm	2	2.25 mm
M/N-13	9 mm	3	2.1 mm
L-11	8 mm	4	2 mm
K-10½	6.5 mm	5	1.9 mm
J-10	6 mm	6	1.8 mm
J-9	5.5 mm	7	1.65 mm
H-8	5 mm	8	1.5 mm
7	4.5 mm	9	1.4 mm
G-6	4 mm	10	1.3 mm
F-5	3.75 mm	11	1.1 mm
E-4	3.5 mm	12	1 mm
D-3	3.25 mm	13	0.85 mm
C-2	2.75 mm	14	0.75 mm
B-1	2.25 mm		

Notions and other materials

You'll need a few other small tools:

- A sewing tape measure to measure gauge swatches and the finished piece
- A yarn needle or tapestry needle to weave in loose ends and assemble some of the projects
- Stitch markers to mark the ends of rows or complicated repetitions
- A pair of sewing scissors

Japanese stole

Pattern on page 33

Cowl

Pattern on page 34

Beret

Pattern on page 36

Shopping bag

Pattern on page 37

Shawl

Pattern on page 39

Tote bag

Pattern on page 40

Fingerless gloves

Pattern on page 43

Oversized scarf

Pattern on page 44

Slippers

Pattern on page 46

Large shopping bag

Pattern on page 47

Hat and matching scarf

Pattern on pages 49 and 50

Cardigan

Pattern on page 51

Sleeveless tunic

Pattern on page 53

Hat

Pattern on page 54

Scarf and belt

Pattern on page 56

Scarf

Pattern on page 57

Purse

Pattern on page 59

Cropped cardigan

Pattern on page 60

Cowl

Pattern on page 62

Necklace

Pattern on page 63

Hexagonal motif

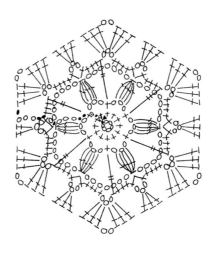

Ch 6, join with sl st in the first ch to form a ring.

Round 1: Ch 1, 12 sc in ring; join with sl st in beginning ch.

Round 2: Ch 1, 1 sc in the first st, *ch 3, skip 1 st, 1 sc in next sc; repeat from * around; join with a sl st in beginning ch.

Round 3: Sl st in first 2 sts, ch 3, dc4tog through first ch-3 sp of prev rnd. *Ch 7, dc5tog in next ch-3 sp; repeat from * around; ch 7, join with sl st in 3rd ch of beginning ch-3.

Round 4: Ch 1; *(sc, ch 3, sc) in next st; in next ch-7 sp, work 4 sc, ch 3, tr in the sc of rnd 2, 3 sc in same ch-7 sp; repeat from * around; join with a sl st in beginning ch.

Round 5: Sl st in the first st, ch 3, 2 dc in first ch-3 sp. *(3 dc, ch 2, 3 dc) in next ch-3 sp, 3 dc in next ch-3 sp; repeat from * around to last ch-3 sp; (3 dc, ch 2, 3 dc) in last ch-3 sp, join with sl st in 3rd ch of beginning ch-3.

Fasten off.

 # Japanese stole

Pattern for motif on p. 32

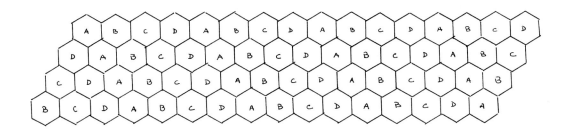

Materials

Super fine acrylic-wool blend yarn
6 skeins (50 g) base color
1 skein (50 g) each contrasting colors A, B, C, and D
Size C-2 (2.75 mm) crochet hook

Size

One size: 12 in. wide x 48 in. long

Gauge

Hexagonal motif = 2¾ in. x 2¾ in.

Motifs needed

The Japanese stole is made of 64 hexagons. For each one, the third round is worked in a contrasting color.

Use the same base color for all the motifs, and make 16 with each contrasting color.

Assembly

Sew the motifs together with a yarn needle (see p. 8).

Follow the diagram above for how to arrange the colors.

Cowl

Pattern for motif on p. 32

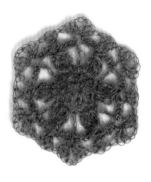

Materials
Lace-weight mohair yarn
3 skeins (25 g)
Size B-1 (2.25 mm) crochet hook

Size
One size: 15 in. tall x 18 in. long

Gauge
Hexagonal motif = 3½ in. x 3½ in.

Motifs needed
Make 60 hexagons (all one color).

Assembly
Sew the motifs together with a yarn needle (see p. 8). Put 12 hexagons together in a row (about 35 in. long). Make 5 rows of hexagons, and sew the rows together. Fold the piece in half lengthwise and sew the two short ends together.

Square motif

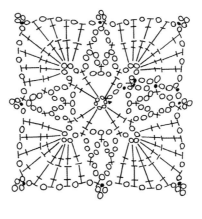

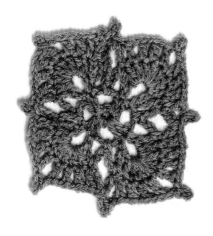

Ch 6, join with sl st to form a ring.

Round 1: Ch 3, dc in ring; (ch 3, 2 dc in ring) 3 times; ch 3, join with sl st in 3rd ch of beginning ch-3.

Round 2: Ch 1, sc in same ch as joining, *ch 5, sc in next dc, ch 5, sc in ch-3 sp, ch 5, sc in next dc; repeat from * around; join with a sl st in the beginning ch.

Round 3: Sl st in same ch as joining, ch 3, 7 dc in next ch-5 sp. *Sc in next ch-5 sp, ch 5, sc in next ch-5 sp,** 8 dc in next ch-5 sp; repeat from * around, ending last repeat at **; join with sl st in 3rd ch of beginning ch-3.

Round 4: Ch 4, in corner shell work (dc in next dc, ch 1) 3 times, p, ch 1, (dc in next dc, ch 1) 4 times. *In next ch-5 sp, (sc, p, ch 1),** (dc in next dc, ch 1) 4 times, p, ch 1, (dc in next dc, ch 1) 4 times; repeat from * around, ending last repeat at **; join with sl st in 3rd ch of beginning ch-4.

Fasten off.

Beret

Pattern for motif on p. 35

A	B	C	B	A
B	C	A	C	B
C	A	B	A	C
B	C	A	C	B
A	B	C	B	A

Materials
Super fine acrylic-wool blend yarn
1 skein (50 g) each colors A, B, and C
Size C-2 (2.75 mm) crochet hook

Size
One size: 11 in. in diameter

Gauge
Square motif = 4 in. x 4 in.

Motifs needed
The beret is made of 25 motifs.
Make 8 motifs in color A, 9 in color B, and 8 in color C.

Assembly
Attach the motifs together with the picot method (see p. 8). As you work the fourth round of every new motif, attach each picot to the next motif with a sl st through the picot on the corresponding side. Assemble the 25 motifs into the base of the beret, following the diagram above for the arrangement of the colors.

Finishing
Join color B on the bottom edge of the beret.

Round 1: Ch 1, 200 dc around the edge of the beret, gently gathering the corners; join with sl st in 3rd ch of beginning ch-3.

Round 2: Ch 3, *dc in next 6 sts, dc2tog (= 1 dec); repeat from * around; join with sl st in 3rd ch of beginning ch-3 (175 sts).

Round 3: Ch 3, *dc in next 5 sts, dc2tog; repeat from * around; join with sl st in 3rd ch of beginning ch-3 (150 sts).

Round 4: Ch 3, *dc in next 4 sts, dc2tog; repeat from * around; join with sl st in 3rd ch of beginning ch-3 (125 sts).

Round 5: Ch 3, *dc in next 3 sts, dc2tog; repeat from * around; join with sl st in 3rd ch of beginning ch-3 (100 sts).

Round 6: Ch 3, *dc in next 2 sts, dc2tog; repeat from * around; join with sl st in 3rd ch of beginning ch-3 (75 sts).

Fasten off.

Shopping bag

Pattern for motif on p. 35

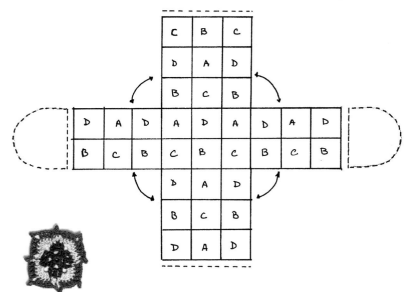

Materials
Light (DK) weight cotton yarn
1 skein (50 g) each colors 1, 2, 3, and 4
2 skeins (50 g) color 5
Size E-4 (3.5 mm) crochet hook

Size
One size: 16 in. wide x 16 in. tall
   (without handles)

Gauge
Square motif = 2¾ in. x 2¾ in.

Motifs needed
The bag is made of 36 squares.
Color pattern A (make 7): Rnds 1 and 2,
   color 2; rnd 3, color 1; rnd 4, color 4.
Color pattern B (make 10): Rnds 1 and 2,
   color 1; rnd 3, color 3; rnd 4, color 5.
Color pattern C (make 8): Rnds 1 and 2,
   color 4; rnd 3, color 2; rnd 4, color 3.
Color pattern D (make 11): Rnds 1 and 2,
   color 5; rnd 3, color 3; rnd 4, color 2.

Assembly
Attach the motifs together with the picot method (see p. 8). As you work the fourth round of every new motif, attach each picot to the next motif with a sl st through the picot on the corresponding side.

Assemble the bag, referring to the diagram above for the arrangement of the colors. Once the cross shape is assembled, attach the sides together (as indicated by the arrows).

Finishing
Join color 5 on the top edge of the bag.

Round 1: Ch 1, 240 sc around top edge of bag; join with sl st in beginning ch.

Rounds 2-4: Ch 1, sc in next st and in each st around; join with sl st in beginning ch.

Fasten off.

For the handles, join color 5 where indicated on the diagram. Ch 80 and join to top edge 50 sts away with a sl st. Work 4 rows of sc along this ch for the handle. Do the same on the opposite side of the bag.

Eight-pointed star motif

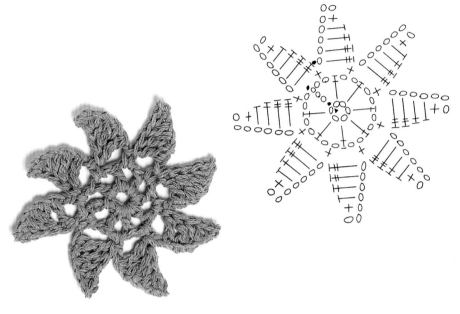

Star motif

Ch 6, join with a sl st to form a ring.

Round 1: Ch 3 (counts as dc), turn; *ch 2, dc through ring; repeat from * 6 more times; ch 2, join with sl st in 3rd ch of beginning ch-3.

Round 2: *Sc in next ch-2 sp, ch 7, on this chain work 1 sc in 3rd ch from hook, hdc in next ch, dc in next ch, tr in each of next 2 chs. Repeat from * around; join with sl st in first sc. Fasten off.

Disk motif (for the bag)

Ch 6, join with sl st to form a ring.

Round 1: Ch 3 (counts as dc), turn; dc through ring, p, *4 dc through ring, p; repeat from * 2 more times, 2 dc through ring; join with sl st in 3rd ch of beginning ch-3. Fasten off.

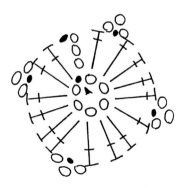

Shawl

Pattern for motif on p. 38

Materials
Super fine acrylic-wool blend yarn
1 skein (50 g) each of 10 different colors
Size C-2 (2.75 mm) crochet hook

Size
One size: 50 in. wide x 28 in. tall

Gauge
Star motif = 2¾ in. x 2¾ in.

Motifs needed
The shawl is made of 32 star motifs of each color, for a total of 320 motifs.

Assembly
Attach the motifs together with the picot method (see p. 8). Attach the stars together as you work by making 1 sl st in the ch at the point of the star on the motif you want to attach the current one to.

Mix up the colors randomly, making sure never to put two stars of the same color next to each other. Start by assembling the longest row, 18 stars; then add the next row of 16 stars, staggering the rows. The third row will have 15 stars, and so on to the point of the shawl.

 # Tote
bag

Pattern for the motifs on p. 38

Materials
Light (DK) weight cotton yarn
2 skeins (50 g) color A
1 skein (50 g) color B
Size E-4 (3.5 mm) crochet hook
Tan canvas or denim fabric, 36 in. x 28 in.
Fabric marker
Sewing thread

Size
One size: 13 in. wide x 15 in. tall

Gauge
Star motif = 4 in. in diameter

Motifs needed
The bag is composed of 32 star motifs—16
in color A and 16 in color B—plus 28
disk motifs in color A.
Alternate the colors when arranging the
stars.

Assembly
Use the picot method to attach the stars
together while you work, attaching each
motif to the next with a sl st through the
ch on the corresponding star point. Then
attach the disk motifs in the same way,
making a sl st through the corresponding
star points as you make the picots. Fold the
completed strip of motifs in half and close
up the bottom and side edges.

Make a single crochet border as follows:
Attach color A at the point of a star of the
same color. *Ch 5, 2 sc in the next point of
the same star, ch 12, 1 sc in the first point
of the next star; repeat from * around; join
with sl st in the first ch of the round. Work
three rounds even in sc. Fasten off.

Canvas lining

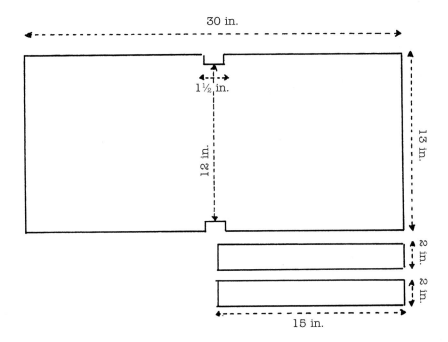

30 in.

13 in.

1½ in.

12 in.

2 in.

2 in.

15 in.

Mark the pieces for the lining and the handles, as indicated above, on a piece of canvas or other thick fabric. Cut out the three pieces, cutting ½ in. outside the lines for a seam allowance.

Sew along the edges of all the pieces with a zigzag stitch.

Fold the piece for the bag in half, with the right side inside, and line up the edges. Pin the edges, then sew them along the lines (½ in. from the edge).

Iron the seams open, then fold each bottom corner of the bag into a T to form a gusset; sew.

Use an iron to fold down and press a double hem of ½ in. around the top opening of the bag. Sew the hem ⅜ in. from the edge. Turn the bag right side out.

Make the handles: Fold to the back and iron the extra ½ in. around the edges of the pieces for the handles. Fold the pieces in half lengthwise, wrong sides (and folded-back material) inside, pin, and then sew ¼ in. from the edges.

To attach the handles, mark the points on the top edge 3½ in. from each side. Place 1 in. of the end of each handle inside the opening of the bag at these points, and baste them to hold them in place. Sew the handles into place ⅜ in. from the edge. To reinforce, sew again in the same place.

Slide the canvas bag inside the crocheted part. Sew around the top edges by hand with sewing thread to attach the two parts of the bag together.

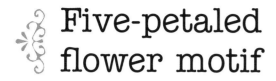

Five-petaled flower motif

Ch 10, join with a sl st to form a ring.

Round 1: *Ch 3, 3 dc through ring, ch 3, sl st through ring; repeat from * 4 more times.

Cut the yarn and fasten off.

Fingerless gloves

Pattern for motif on p. 42

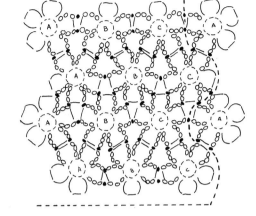

repeated pattern

Materials
Lace-weight mohair yarn
1 skein (25 g) each of colors A, B, and C
Size B-1 (2.25 mm) crochet hook

Size
One size

Gauge
Flower motif = 3.2 in. in diameter

Motifs needed
One fingerless glove is composed of 63 flower motifs, 21 in each
    of the three colors. Alternate the colors, distributing them
    evenly through the piece, as indicated in the diagram.
For one glove, make a rectangle 7 flowers wide by 9 flowers long.

Assembly
Attach the flowers to each other as you make them by working
a sl st in each of the sts on the end of each petal of an adjoining
flower, as indicated in the diagram.

Finishing
Fold the rectangle in half and attach the sides together as
previously. Leave an opening two flowers from the end of the
mitten for the thumb hole (about 2¾ in.).
    Make the second glove the same way as the first.

Oversized scarf

Pattern for motif on p. 42

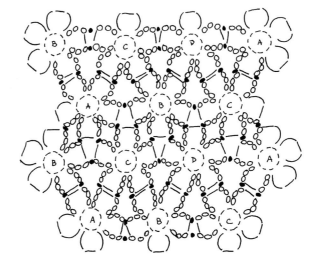

Materials
Super bulky weight velour yarn
5 skeins (50 g) each colors A, B, C, and D
Size N/P-15 (10 mm) crochet hook

Size
One size: 16 in. wide x 83 in. long

Gauge
Flower motif = 4¾ in. in diameter

Motifs needed
The scarf is made of 73 flower motifs, 21 in color A, 21 in color B, 21 in color C, and 10 in color D. Alternate the colors and distribute them evenly through the scarf, as indicated in the diagram above.

Assembly
Attach the flowers to each other as you make them by working a sl st in each of the sts on the end of each petal of an adjoining flower, as indicated in the diagram.

The scarf is made up of two repeated rows; one row of four motifs and another of three motifs.

Square rosette motif

Ch 6, join with sl st to form a ring.

Round 1: Ch 5, *dc in ring, ch 2; repeat from * 6 more times; join with a sl st in 3rd ch of beginning ch-5.

Round 2: Ch 1, (sc, hdc, 3 dc, hdc, sc) in next ch-2 sp and in every ch-2 sp around (8 petals); join with a sl st in beginning ch.

Round 3: *Ch 5 (place this ch behind the petal made in the prev rnd), 1 sc in the next dc of rnd 1; repeat from * 7 more times; join with sl st in first ch of beginning ch-5.

Round 4: (Sc, hdc, 5 dc, hdc, sc) in next ch-5 sp and in each ch-5 sp around (8 petals); join with a sl st in first sc.

Round 5: *Ch 5 (place this ch behind the petal made in the prev rnd), 1 sc in the next sc of rnd 3; repeat from * 7 more times; join with sl st in first ch of beginning ch-5.

Round 6: (Sc, hdc, 7 dc, hdc, sc) in next ch-5 sp and in each ch-5 sp around (8 petals); join with a sl st in first sc. Fasten off.

Round 7: Join yarn at the top of one of the petals with a sl st, ch 1, sc in next st, *ch 5, (dtr3tog, ch 3, dtr3tog, ch 3, dtr3tog) in 4th dc of next petal, ch 5, sc in the 4th dc of next petal; repeat from * around; join with sl st in beginning ch.

Round 8: Ch 3, dc in next st, ch 1, dc in next 3 sts, *ch 1, 3 dc in next ch-3 sp, (3 dc, ch 3, 3 dc) in corner st, ch 1, 3 dc in next ch-3 sp, ch 1, sk next st and ch, dc in next 3 sts, ch 1,** dc in next 3 sts, ch 1, dc in next 3 sts; repeat from * around, ending last repeat at **; dc in next st; join with sl st in 3rd ch of beginning ch-3. Fasten off.

Slippers

Pattern for motif on p. 45

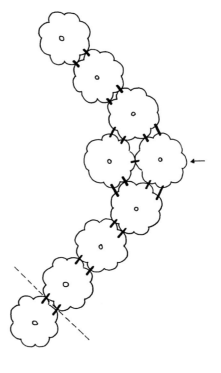

Materials
Sport-weight alpaca yarn
1 skein (50 g) each colors A and B
Size C-2 (2.75 mm) crochet hook
Tan wool felt, 8 in. x 12 in.
Rotary cutter or sharp scissors
Sewing thread

Sizes
Small (shoe size 4–7)
Large (shoe size 8–10)

Gauge
Rosette motif (without square) = 2½ in. in diameter

Motifs needed
The slippers are made from just the rosette part of the motif
    (rounds 1–6). Use color A for rounds 1–2 and color B for
    rounds 3–6.
For small size, make 8 rosettes; for large size, make 9 rosettes.

Assembly
Make the motifs, then sew them together with a yarn needle.
Sew the petals together as indicated in the diagram. For the large
size, add an extra rosette on one side. Fold the assembled piece in
half and sew the petals on the ends together.

Finishing
Trace the foot template (see the templates on p. 64) twice on
the back of the felt. Cut the pieces out. Pin the crocheted piece
along the edge of the felt piece and sew them together with small
stitches through the outer petals of the rosettes.

Large shopping bag

Pattern for motif on p. 45

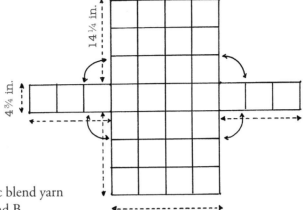

14¼ in.

4¾ in.

19 in.

Materials
Light (DK) weight wool-acrylic blend yarn
8 skeins (50 g) each colors A and B
Size G-6 (4 mm) crochet hook
Black denim or canvas fabric for the lining, 36 in. x 151 in.
Fabric marker
Sewing thread
A pair of black leather (or imitation leather) handles, 28 in. x 1 in.

Size
One size: 19 in. wide x 14 in. tall x 4¾ in. deep

Gauge
Flower motif = 4¾ in. x 4¾ in.

Motifs needed
The bag is made up of 34 squares.
Use color A for round 1, color B for rounds 2–6, and color A for
    rounds 7 and 8.

Assembly
Make the 34 squares, then use the crochet method (see p. 8) to
assemble them, working a single row of single crochet with color
A along all the seams between motifs. Assemble the squares as
illustrated in the diagram.

Finishing
Trace the shape of the bag onto a piece of black canvas. Cut
around the piece, ⅜ in. outside the traced lines. Sew the side
seams ⅜ in. from the edge.

Fold over ⅜ in. along the opening of the canvas bag, and sew
this hem. Pin the ends of the handles 4 in. from the side seams
and sew them several times to solidly attach them.

Slide the lining inside the crocheted bag and sew the edges of
the crocheted bag to the lining by hand with very small stitches.

Overlapping squares motif

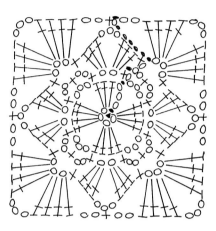

Ch 4, join with sl st to form a ring.

Round 1: Ch 3, 3 dc in ring, *ch 3, 4 dc in ring; repeat from * 2 more times, ch 3, sl st in 3rd ch of beginning ch-3.

Round 2: Ch 1, sc in same st as joining, *ch 2, sk next 2 dc, sc in next dc, ch 2, sc in next ch-3 sp, ch 2, sc in next dc; repeat from * around, join with sl st in beginning ch.

Round 3: Ch 1, *(3 dc, ch 3, 3 dc) in next ch-2 sp, sc in next ch-2 sp, ch 3,** sc in next ch-2 sp; repeat from * around, ending last repeat at **; join with sl st in beginning ch.

Round 4: Sl st in first 5 sts, ch 1, *sc in next ch-3 sp, ch 2, (4 dc, ch 3, 4 dc) in next ch-3 sp, ch 2; repeat from * around; join with sl st in first sc.

Fasten off.

Hat

Pattern for motif on p. 48

A	A	A	A	A	A	A	A	A	A
A	A	A	A	A	A	A	A	A	A
A	A	A	A	A	A	A	A	A	A
C	C	C	C	C	C	C	C	C	C

Materials
Sport-weight alpaca yarn
2 skeins (50 g) color A
1 skein (50 g) color C
Size C-2 (2.75 mm) crochet hook

Size
One size

Gauge
Square motif = 2¼ in. x 2¼ in.

Motifs needed
The hat is made up of 40 squares, 30 in color A and 10 in color C.

Assembly
Make all the squares, then sew them together with a yarn needle (see p. 8), following the arrangement in the diagram above.

Finishing
Fold the piece in half and sew the short ends together. With color A, make a twisted cord about 40 in. long: Cut 180 in. of yarn, fold it in half, and put the end with the loop around a doorknob or other support. Twist the strands of yarn clockwise. When the yarn is well twisted, fold it in half again and let it twist up on itself. Detach the loop end from the doorknob and knot all four strands of the cord together at this end to keep it from unraveling.

Thread the twisted cord through the holes in the motifs about half a square from the top of the hat. Pull to gather the top of the hat and tie the cord.

Matching scarf

Pattern for motif on p. 48

B	B	B	B
A	A	A	A
C	C	C	C
A	A	A	A
B	B	B	B
A	A	A	A
C	C	C	C
A	A	A	A
B	B	B	B
A	A	A	A
C	C	C	C
A	A	A	A
B	B	B	B
A	A	A	A
C	C	C	C
A	A	A	A
B	B	B	B
A	A	A	A
C	C	C	C
A	A	A	A
B	B	B	B

Materials
Sport-weight alpaca yarn
2 skeins (50 g) color A
1 skein (50 g) color B
1 skein (50 g) color C
Size C-2 (2.75 mm) crochet
   hook

Size
One size

Gauge
Square motif = 2¼ in. x 2¼ in.

Motifs needed
The scarf is made of 84 squares:
40 in color A, 24 in color B,
and 20 in color C.

Assembly
Sew the squares together (see p.
8), following the arrangement
given in the diagram.

Cardigan

Pattern for motif on p. 48

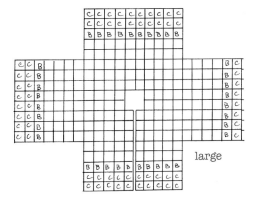

small

medium

large

Materials

Sport-weight alpaca yarn

6 skeins (50 g) color A for small and
medium, 7 skeins for large

1 skein (50 g) color B for all sizes

2 skeins (50 g) color C for all sizes

Size C-2 (2.75 mm) crochet hook

Sizes

Small (4–6), medium (8–10), and large (12–14)

Gauge

Square motif = 2¼ in. x 2¼ in.

Motifs needed

The small cardigan requires 208 squares: 112 in color A, 32 in
color B, and 64 in color C.

The medium cardigan requires 224 squares: 128 in color A, 32
in color B, and 64 in color C.

The large cardigan requires 292 squares: 196 in color A, 32 in
color B, and 64 in color C.

Assembly

Make the required number of motifs and arrange them as
indicated in the diagrams above. Sew the motifs together with a
yarn needle (see p. 8).

Medallion motif

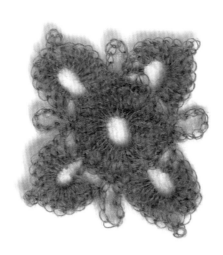

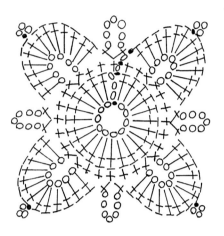

Ch 10, join with sl st to form a ring.

Round 1: Ch 3, 23 dc in ring, join with sl st in 3rd ch of beginning ch-3.

Round 2: Ch 1, sc in same ch as joining, sc in next 2 sts, then *(sc, ch 7, sc) in next st,** sc in next 5 sts; repeat from * around, ending last repeat at **, sc in next 2 sts, sl st in beginning ch.

Round 3: Ch 1, (sc, ch 7, sc) in first st, *(7 dc, p, 7 dc) in next ch-7 sp, sk next 2 sts, (sc, ch 7, sc) in next st, sk next 2 sts; repeat from * around, (7 dc, p, 7 dc) in last ch-7 sp; join with sl st in beginning ch.

Fasten off.

Assembly diagram

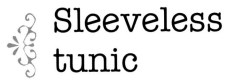 # Sleeveless tunic

Pattern for motif on p. 52

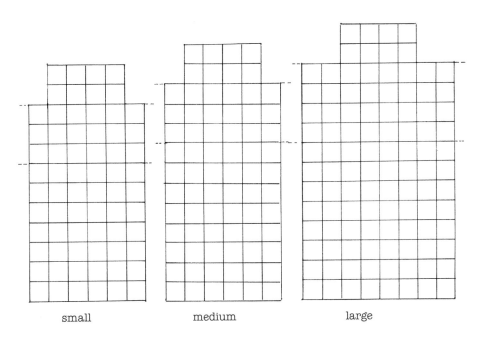

small   medium   large

Materials

Light (DK) weight wool-acrylic blend yarn
11 skeins (50 g) for small size
12 skeins for medium
15 skeins for large
Size E-4 (3.5 mm) crochet hook

Sizes

Small (4–6), medium (8–10), and
large (12–14)

Gauge

Medallion motif = 2¾ in. x 2¾ in.

Motifs needed

Make 68 squares for the small tunic, 74
for the medium tunic, or 104 for the large
tunic.

Assembly

Use the picot method (see p. 8) to assemble
the motifs as you make them, working sl
sts in the points of the petals and in the
larger side loop of the neighboring motifs
as you work the last round on each new
motif (see the diagram on p. 52).

Following the diagrams above, make a
back and a front in the desired size.

Attach the back of the garment to the
front by working sl sts through the petal
picots and side loops. Leave the spaces
between the dotted lines in the diagrams
above open for sleeve holes.

Hat

Pattern for motif on p. 52

Materials
Lace-weight mohair yarn
1 skein (25 g)
Size B-1 (2.25 mm) crochet hook

Size
One size

Gauge
Medallion motif = 2¾ in. x 2¾ in.

Motifs needed
The hat is made of 21 motifs arranged in a rectangle, 3 squares by 7 squares.

Assembly
Use the picot method (see p. 8) to assemble the motifs as you make them, working sl sts in the points of the petals and in the larger side loop of the neighboring motifs as you work the last round on each new motif (see the diagram on p. 52).

Join the motifs into a 3 x 7 rectangle, then fold the rectangle in half and join the short ends to make a tube.

Finishing
Edging
Join the yarn at the base of a petal and work around the bottom edge of the piece as follows:

Round 1: Ch 1, *5 sc along petal (working away from center of motif), work 1 sc in the picots joining the two motifs, 5 sc along next petal, ch 2, sc in the next 7-ch sp; repeat from * around (6 more times); join with sl st in the beginning ch.

Rounds 2–4: Ch 3, dc in next st and in each st around; join with sl st in 3rd ch of beginning ch-3.

Fasten off.

Top of hat
Join the yarn at the tip of a petal and work around the top edge of the piece as follows:

Round 1: Ch 3, *3 dc along the edge of the petal (working toward the center of the motif), dc in next ch-7 sp, 3 dc along next petal; repeat from * around (6 more times); join with sl st in 3rd ch of beginning ch-3.

Rounds 2 and 3: Ch 3, *dc in next 2 sts, dc2tog; repeat from * around.

At the end of round 3, cut the yarn and fasten off, leaving a long tail. Thread the tail through the sts of the last round and tighten. Fasten off and weave in the end.

Six-petaled flower motif

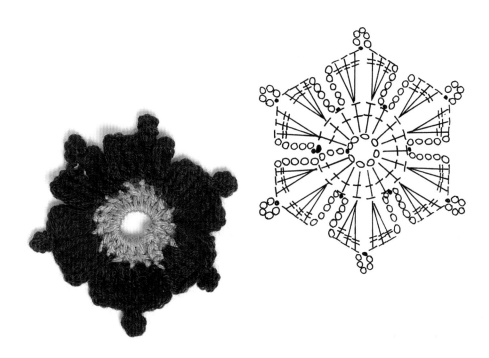

Ch 8, join with sl st to form a ring.

Round 1: Ch 3, 17 dc in ring, join with sl st in 3rd ch of beginning ch-3.

Round 2: *Ch 5, 3 tr in next st, work a 5-ch picot, 3 tr in next st, ch 5, sl st in next st; repeat from * around.

Fasten off.

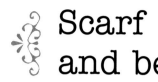

Scarf and belt

Pattern for motif on p. 55

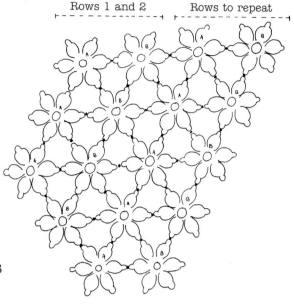

Rows 1 and 2   Rows to repeat

Materials
Super fine acrylic-wool blend yarn
3 skeins (50 g) each colors A and B
2 skeins (50 g) color C
Size C-2 (2.75 mm) crochet hook

Size
One size: 13 in. wide x 80 in. long

Gauge
Flower motif = 2¾ in. in diameter

Motifs needed
The scarf is made of 61 motifs in color A and 58 in color B (119 motifs in all); work round 1 in color C for all motifs, and round 2 in color A or B.
For a belt of about 48 in., you will need 12 motifs each in colors A and B.

Assembly
Use the picot method (see p. 8) to attach the motifs to each other as you make them, working a sl st through the picot of the next motif's petal as you work the picots of the second round. Follow the diagram above for the arrangement of the colors. Start at the point of the scarf, with a row of 3 flowers in color A, then a row of 4 flowers in color B; continue by alternating rows of 5 flowers in A and B. Finish the scarf with a row of 4 flowers in color B and a row of 3 flowers in color A.

To make the belt, make a single strip of 12 flower motifs, alternating between color A and color B, each attached to the next at just one point.

 # Scarf

Pattern for motif on p. 55

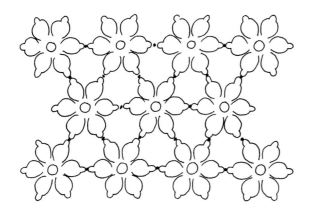

Materials
Lace-weight mohair yarn
1 skein (25 g) color A
2 skeins (25 g) color B
Size B-1 (2.25 mm) crochet hook

Size
One size: 10 in. wide x 40 in. long

Gauge
Flower motif = $2\frac{1}{2}$ in. in diameter

Motifs needed
The scarf is made of 53 motifs. Work round 1 of each flower in color A and round 2 in color B.

Assembly
Use the picot method (see p. 8) to attach the motifs to each other as you make them, working a sl st through the picot of the next motif's petal as you work the picots of the second round. Start with a row of 4 flowers, then stagger the next row, which will only have 3 flowers; continue to alternate rows of 3 and 4 flowers (8 rows of 4 and 7 of 3). The first and last rows should each have 4 flowers.

Square flower motif

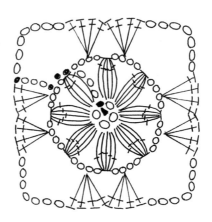

Ch 4, join with a sl st to form a ring.

Round 1: Ch 3, dc4tog in ring, *ch 4, dc5tog in ring; repeat from * 6 more times; join with sl st in 3rd ch of beginning ch-3.

Round 2: Sl st in first 2 chs, ch 3, 3 dc in this ch-4 sp; *4 dc in next ch-4 sp, ch 7,** 4 dc in next ch-4 sp; repeat from * around, ending last repeat at **; join with sl st in 3rd ch of beginning ch-3.

Fasten off.

Purse

Pattern for motif on p. 58

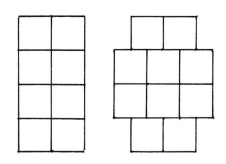

Materials

Light (DK) weight wool-acrylic blend yarn

1 skein (50 g) for small purse, or use 1 skein each colors A, B, C, D, and E

1 skein (50 g) each colors D and F for large purse

Size E-4 (3.5 mm) crochet hook

Small version: 1 purse clasp frame (ready to assemble, with holes to sew through), 4¾ in. wide

Large version: 1 purse clasp frame (ready to assemble, with holes to sew through), 6 in. wide

Black felt, 20 in. square

Pearl cotton to match the yarn used

Light-colored fabric pencil

Ruler

Scissors

Size

Small version: 5 in. wide x 5½ in. tall

Large version: 7 in. wide x 5 in. tall

Gauge

Square motif = 2½ in. x 2½ in.

Motifs needed

The small version is made of 8 squares and the large version of 10 squares.

For a multicolored small purse, make the motifs in the following color combinations:

Round 1, color A; round 2, color B—make 2

Round 1, color A; round 2, color C—make 2

Round 1, color A; round 2, color D—make 2

Round 1, color A; round 2, color E—make 2

For the large purse, make all the motifs in the following color combination: round 1, color D; round 2, color F.

Assembly

Sew the motifs together with a yarn needle (see p. 8).

For the small version, make a rectangle 2 squares by 4 squares. Fold in half and sew the sides together, leaving the top open.

For the large version, make a row of 3 squares and a row of 2 squares, then center the short row along the top of the long row and sew the two together (see the diagram above). Make the second side of the purse in the same way. Sew the side and bottom seams.

Lining

Use a ruler and a fabric pencil to trace the lining pattern on the felt. Cut out the pieces ¼ in. from the lines.

For the small purse, fold the rectangle in half and sew along the marked lines. Turn so that the seams are in the inside. Slip the lining inside the crocheted purse. Open the clasp frame and sew both the lining and the crocheted outer part to the frame with pearl cotton, sewing in back stitch through the holes in the frame. Sew the second side of the purse and lining to the clasp in the same way.

For the large purse, sew the sides and bottom edge of the lining together, sewing along the marked lines. Assemble the lining, outer part, and clasp as for the small purse.

Cropped cardigan

Pattern for motif on p. 58

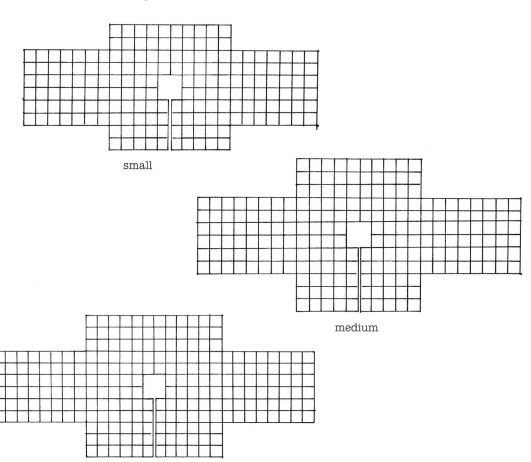

small

medium

large

Materials
Light (DK) weight cotton yarn
8 skeins (50 g) for small and medium,
    10 skeins for large
Size E-4 (3.5 mm) crochet hook

Sizes
Small (4–6), medium (8–10), and
large (12–14)

Gauge
Square motif = 2¼ in. x 2¼ in.

Motifs needed
Small size: Make 180 motifs.
Medium size: Make 192 motifs.
Large size: Make 236 motifs.

Assembly
Use a yarn needle to sew the motifs
together (see p. 8) in the arrangement
indicated in the diagrams above. Sew the
sleeve and side seams.

Six-pointed star motif

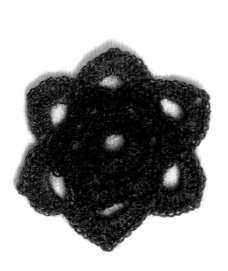

Ch 8, join with sl st to form a ring.

Round 1: Ch 3, 23 dc in ring; join with sl st in 3rd ch of beginning ch-3.

Round 2: Ch 1, sc in same ch as joining, *ch 3, sk next dc, sc in next dc; repeat from * around; join with sl st in beginning ch.

Round 3: Ch 1, *sc in next ch-3 sp, 7 dc in next ch-3 sp; repeat from * around; join with sl st in beginning ch.

Round 4: Sl st in first 2 sts, ch 1, *sc in the 2nd dc of next shell, ch 3, sk next 3 dc, sc in next dc, ch 5; repeat from * around; join with sl st in beginning ch.

Round 5: Sl st in first 2 sts, ch 1, *sc in next ch-3 sp, (6 dc, ch 2, 6 dc) in next ch-3 sp; repeat from * around; join with sl st in beginning ch.

Fasten off.

Cowl

Pattern for motif on p. 61

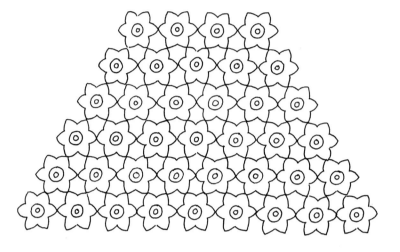

Materials
Lace-weight mohair yarn
2 skeins (25 g) color A
3 skeins (25 g) color B
Size B-1 (2.25 mm) crochet hook

Size
One size: 20 in. around at widest point x
12 in. tall

Gauge
Star motif = 2¼ in. in diameter

Motifs needed
The cowl is made of 78 motifs. Work each
motif in the following colors: rounds 1–3
in color A; rounds 4–5 in color B.

Assembly
Use the picot technique to attach the stars
to each other as you make them, working a
sl st in each of the ch-2 spaces at the points
of the neighboring stars as you make each
new motif.

The cowl is made in two parts: the front
and the back.

Following the diagram above, start with
a row of 9 stars; staggering the rows, add a
row of 8 stars, then a row of 7, and so on
until you have 6 rows, with 4 stars in the
shortest row.

Make the other side of the cowl the
same way.

Finishing
Once you have completed the two parts of
the cowl, put them together with wrong
sides together. Use a yarn needle threaded
with color B to sew the stars on the ends of
the rows together at their points.

Necklace

Pattern for motif on p. 61

Materials
Lace-weight cotton or linen yarn
Size 8 (1.5 mm) steel crochet hook

Size
One size: 16 in. long

Gauge
Flower = 1 in. in diameter
Circle = ½ in. in diameter

Pattern
The necklace is made of 8 lengths of chain stitch, to which the flower and circle motifs are attached. The flower is rounds 1–3 of the six-pointed star motif, and the circle is rounds 1 and 2. Make 3 flowers and 8 circles.

Strand 1 (make 1): Ch 100, sl st in the edge of a circle motif, ch 50, sl st in a petal of a flower motif, ch 5, sl st in the next petal of the same flower, ch 70, sl st in the edge of a circle, ch 30, sl st in the edge of a circle, ch 50. Join with a sl st in the first ch and fasten off.

Strand 2 (make 1): Ch 60, sl st in the edge of a circle, ch 30, sl st in the edge of a circle, 80 sl st in a petal of a flower, ch 5, sl st in the next petal of the same flower, ch 60. Join with a sl st in the first ch and fasten off.

Strand 3 (make 1): Ch 80, sl st in the edge of a circle, ch 30, sl st in a petal of a flower, ch 5, sl st in the next petal of the same flower, ch 50, sl st in the edge of a circle, ch 20, sl st in the edge of a circle, ch 100. Join with a sl st in the first ch and fasten off.

Strand 4 (make 5): Ch 300. Join with a sl st in the first ch and fasten off.

Assembly
Gently iron or block the strands of the necklace. Put them together so they all fall at about the same level. Twist the strands together over a length of 1 in. and use a sewing needle to sew them together. Weave any loose ends into the bundle of necklaces.

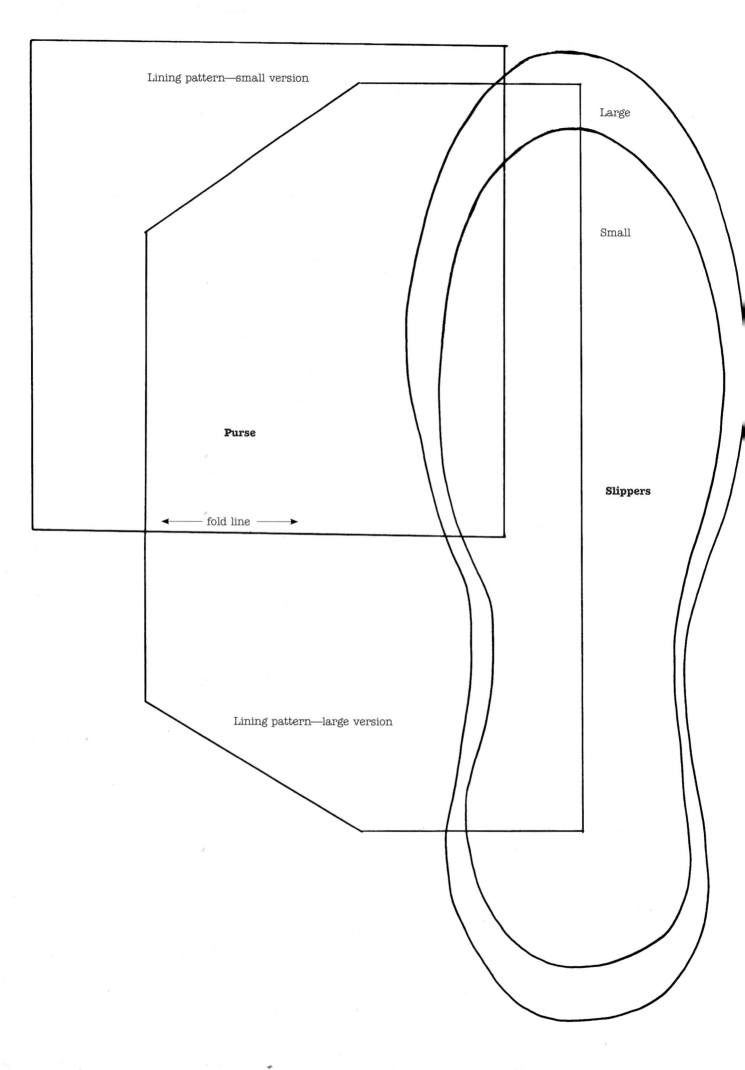

Lining pattern—small version

Large

Small

Purse

Slippers

← fold line →

Lining pattern—large version